Moons and Rings
COMPANIONS TO THE PLANETS

An Earlybird Book
by Jeanne Bendick

Illustrated by Mike Roffe

THE MILLBROOK PRESS INC.

BROOKFIELD, CONNECTICUT

Cataloging-in-Publication Data

Bendick, Jeanne
Moons and rings: companions to the planets/by Jeanne Bendick
32p.; ill.: (Early Bird Books)
Includes index
Summary: Simple answers to children's questions about the moon.
What is it made of? What does it do? What keeps it up in the sky? Do
other planets have a moon? What are rings?
ISBN 1-56294-000-7
1. Moon. 2. Lunar geology. 3. Solar system. 4. Planets. I. Title. II.
Title: Companions to the planets. III. Series.
1991
523.3 BEN

Published by The Millbrook Press Inc, 2 Old New Milford Road, Brookfield,
Connecticut 06804, USA

Produced by Eagle Books Limited, Vigilant House, 120 Wilton Road,
London SW1V 1JZ, England

Contents

full Moon

half Moon

Earth's Moon

Wherever you live on Earth, you can see the Moon.

A full Moon looks like a round dish.

A half Moon looks like half a dish.

A crescent Moon might look like a smile in the sky.

crescent Moon   new Moon

When the Moon is in the sky but you can't see it, that's called a **new Moon.**

However it looks, the Moon is always round. All the shapes you see — plus the new Moon, which you can't see — are called the **phases** of the Moon.

5

What Is Moonlight?

The full Moon is very bright. But the Moon has no light of its own. The Moon shines because light from the Sun shines on it and the Moon reflects that light. So moonlight is really reflected sunlight!

The Sun is always shining on the Moon, but as the Moon goes around the Earth, we see different parts of it lit up.

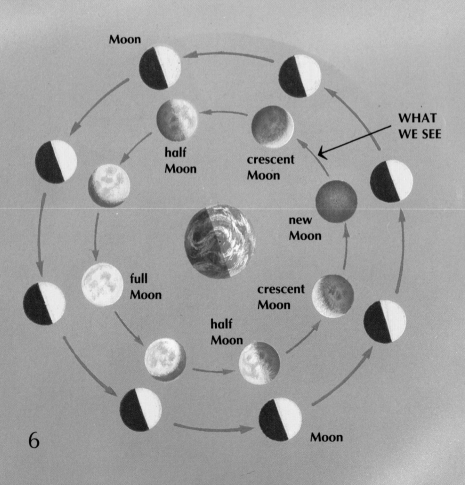

Moon

half Moon

crescent Moon

WHAT WE SEE

new Moon

full Moon

crescent Moon

half Moon

Moon

When you can see only part of the Moon, it's because the Sun is shining only on that part. When the Moon is dark, the Sun is not shining on any part you can see.

The Moon Is a Satellite

Our Moon is a **satellite** of Earth, the planet we live on. A satellite is an object that travels in a special path around another object in space. This path is called an **orbit.**

The Earth and the other planets are all satellites of our star, the Sun. It takes a year for the Earth to travel in its orbit around the Sun.

It takes about 28 days for the Moon to orbit the Earth. That's about a month. In a month we see all the phases of the Moon.

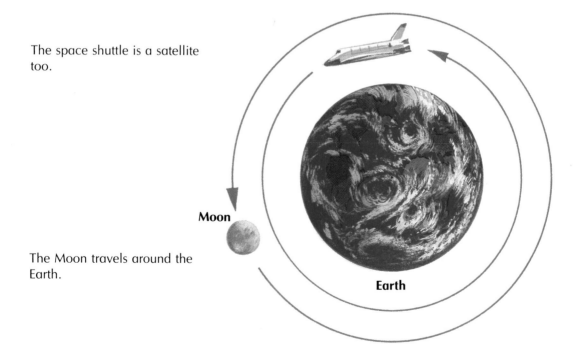

The space shuttle is a satellite too.

The Moon travels around the Earth.

Moon

Earth

8

The Earth's gravity keeps the Moon in orbit.

The Sun's gravity keeps the planets in orbit.

What Keeps a Satellite in Orbit?

Gravity keeps satellites in orbit. Gravity is a force that pulls things toward each other.

The Sun's gravity keeps the planets in orbit.

The Earth's gravity keeps you from falling off into space. It also keeps the Moon in orbit.

high tide

The Moon has gravity, too. The Moon's gravity pulls on Earth, but you hardly notice it. What you can notice is the Moon's gravity pulling on the Earth's oceans, making the level of the water rise and fall. These changes are called the **tides.** The Moon's gravity causes high tides and low tides all over our planet.

low tide

The Moon and the Earth

Scientists think that the Earth and its Moon were formed at the same time, about 4½ billion years ago. In the beginning they might have been alike except for size. But now the Earth and Moon are very different from each other.

Or, something might have crashed into the Earth after it was formed. A part of the Earth broke off and flew out into space, to become the Moon.

The Earth has an atmosphere, the air around us.

It has a blue sky. Sunlight and air together make the sky look blue.

The Earth has water. It has rivers, oceans, rain, and clouds.

Because there are air and water, plants and animals can live on the Earth. Living things need air and water.

On Earth, trees rustle. Birds sing. Animals bark or meow or roar. People shout. Cars honk. Water splashes. Air carries all those sounds.

The Moon has no air. There is no air to make the sky blue, so the sky is always black. There is no air to make wind and no water to make clouds or rain.

There is no air to carry sound, so the Moon is always silent.

14

Because there is no air or water, there are no plants or animals on the Moon. Nothing grows on the Moon. Nothing lives there. When astronauts go to the Moon, they bring air to breathe. They also bring water to drink and food to eat.

The Moon is a brown and dusty desert.
It has big holes where rocks from space have crashed into it. The holes are called **craters.** Sometimes space rocks head for Earth, too. But usually our atmosphere slows them down and burns them up before they reach the ground. The Moon has no atmosphere to do that.

If you were standing on the Moon, Earth would look like this to you.

When you look carefully at the Moon you can see both light and dark places. The lighter places are mountains, pushed up billions of years ago. The darker places are flat plains.

Would it be fun to have
a sky full of moons?

Earth has only one Moon. But some planets in
the Solar System, our neighborhood in space, have
many moons. Two planets have no moons.

Mercury, the planet closest to the Sun, has no
moon. Venus, the next planet from the Sun, has no
moon. Earth, the third planet, has one. Mars, the
next planet beyond Earth, has two.

18

The Moons of Mars

The moons of Mars are very small. They seem to be just brown, lumpy rocks that look like orbiting potatoes. Their names are Deimos and Phobos.

The name of our moon is Moon. Most moons in the Solar System are named after people in ancient myths. A few moons are named after characters in plays or books.

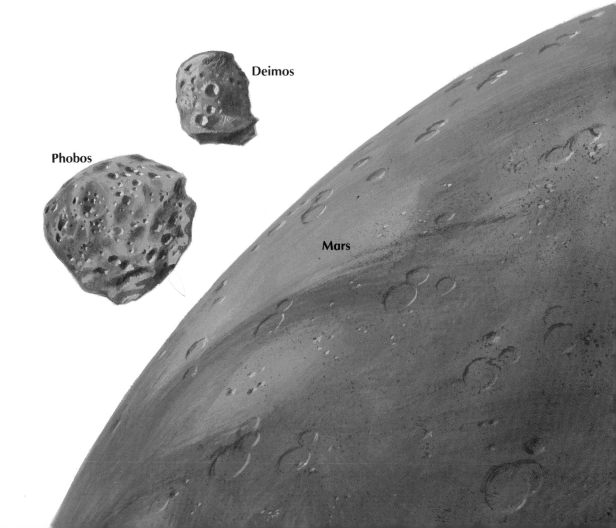

Deimos

Phobos

Mars

The Moons of Jupiter

The planet past Mars is the giant planet Jupiter, which has at least 16 moons. They are different from our Moon and different from each other.

Four of them are very big. Those moons were first seen almost 400 years ago when the scientist Galileo built his telescope for looking at the sky.

Jupiter

Ganymede

Ganymede, orbiting Jupiter, is the largest moon in the Solar System. It is bigger than our Moon and bigger than the planets Mercury and Pluto. The surface of Ganymede is dark and rocky, with ice that is wrinkled up into long ridges. There are also polar ice caps, like the ice at the North Pole and South Pole of the Earth.

Ganymede

Callisto

Callisto is another of Jupiter's big moons. Its dark, sooty surface has more craters than any other moon in the Solar System. In some places there are giant bull's-eyes around the craters. Under the soot, Callisto's surface is ice.

Io

Jupiter's moon Io is almost exactly the same size as Earth's Moon. It may be the most unusual moon in the Solar System. Why?

Io has volcanoes! Earth has a few volcanoes that erupt once in a while. Io has many volcanoes, and some of them are erupting all the time. The surface of Io looks like a calico cat. It is orange, red, and yellow, with white patches and black spots. The black spots are volcanoes that aren't erupting at the moment.

Io's shape is odd, too. It keeps changing, like silly putty. Jupiter pulls on it from one direction and the moons Ganymede and Europa pull on it from other directions.

Io

Callisto

Europa

Europa

Europa is the fourth largest of
Jupiter's moons. It is almost the same
size as our Moon. Europa's surface is
covered with cracked ice that floats
on water. It looks like a ping-pong
ball with scribbles on it.

23

Jupiter's four big moons have almost circular orbits around Jupiter. So do some smaller ones that are closer to the planet. Farther away, another group of moons orbit in the opposite direction. Some of their paths crisscross each other. The farthest moons orbit in the same direction as the inner moons.

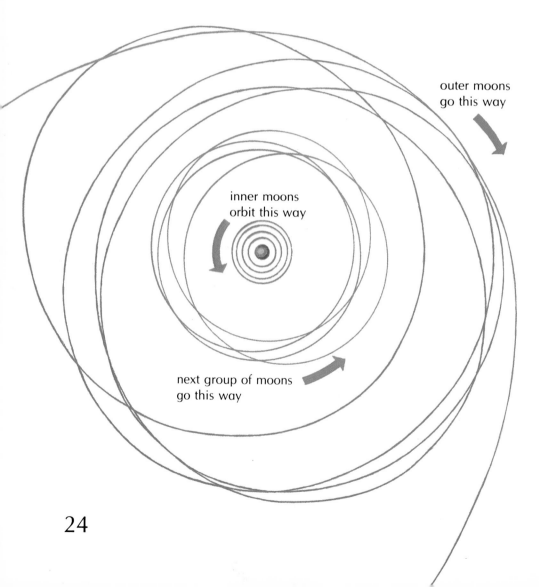

outer moons
go this way

inner moons
orbit this way

next group of moons
go this way

A Ring Around Jupiter

In addition to its moons, Jupiter has a bright, narrow ring around it. The ring is as thin as a wisp of smoke. Scientists think it is made of very tiny particles that are being yanked away from a small moon at the edge of the ring.

The Moons and Rings of Saturn

Saturn, the largest planet after Jupiter, has at least 20 moons. But Saturn's rings are the most exciting thing about it. Galileo discovered them when he looked at Saturn through his telescope.

Saturn looks like a yellowish ball, floating in the center of its rings. There are hundreds and hundreds of rings. Some are wide. Some are narrow. Some are broken. Some are braided. The rings seem to be made of particles of ice and rock. They come in many sizes. Some are the size of marbles. Some are as big as soccer balls. A few are big enough to be tiny moons.

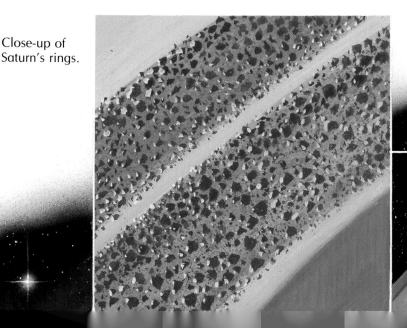

Close-up of Saturn's rings.

Astronomers, scientists who study stars and planets, aren't sure where Saturn's rings came from. Maybe the rings are made of matter left over when the planet was formed. Maybe they were once several small moons that crashed together and broke into many pieces. Maybe they were once a moon that was pulled to pieces or broken up by a passing comet.

Saturn's gravity holds the rings in place. Also, some of the small moons act as shepherds, keeping pieces from wandering out of their orbits.

Earth's Moon

Titan

Titan

Saturn's moon Titan is the second largest moon in the Solar System. It is bigger than the planets Mercury and Pluto. Titan has its own atmosphere, a thick orange smog. Some scientists think that the clouds at the top of the atmosphere might rain a sort of icy gasoline onto Titan's frozen, swampy surface.

Saturn's Other Moons

Saturn's moons, too, are different from each other, but they seem to be made mostly of rock covered with thick ice. One moon has a bright white side and a very black side. One gray moon moves backward. Two small moons chase each other. First one gets ahead, then the other does.

The Moons and Rings of Uranus

Beyond Saturn is the planet Uranus, which has five big moons and ten smaller ones. The two largest moons, Oberon and Titania, are about half the size of our Moon. Uranus also has rings. They are almost black. As the rings orbit their planet, they are kept in place by very small, dark moons that seem to act as traffic police.

Uranus, the third largest planet, rotates on its side. It has fifteen moons and eleven rings.

The Moons and Rings of Neptune

Most of the time, Neptune is the eighth planet from the Sun. Sometimes, though, its orbit takes it outside the orbit of the farthest planet, Pluto.

Neptune has eight known moons and some faint rings. Triton is the biggest moon, a little larger than our Moon. Triton has a thin, pale pink atmosphere. Triton also has volcanoes, but they spit ice, not fire.

Triton is the only big moon in the Solar System that orbits its planet backward. It is slowly drifting in toward Neptune. Scientists think that in a million years or so it will either crash into Neptune or break up into a ring around it.

Triton

Neptune

Charon

Pluto and Charon

Pluto

Pluto is usually the farthest planet from the Sun. It is a tiny planet, smaller than any of the big moons. But even tiny Pluto has a moon of its own, called Charon. Charon is about half the size of its planet.

Some scientists think that Pluto and Charon form a double planet system, with the planets orbiting each other. Some even think that Pluto and Charon might have once been moons of Neptune that were yanked out of their orbits.

Are there moons in our Solar System that we don't know about yet? There might be some small ones. Are there moons around other planets orbiting other stars? Nobody knows yet. But we're looking!

Index